501
Synonym & Antonym Questions

501

Synonym & Antonym Questions

LEARNINGEXPRESS

NEW YORK

Library of Congress Cataloging-in-Publication Data:
Dermott, Brigit.
    501 synonym and antonym questions / Brigit Dermott.— 1st ed.
       p. cm.
    ISBN 1-57685-423-X (pbk.)
    1. English language—Examinations—Study guides. 2. English language—
Synonyms and antonyms—Problems, exercises, etc. I. Title: Five hundred
one synonym and antonym questions. II. Title: Five hundred and one
synonym and antonym questions. III. Title.
    LB1631.5 .D47 2002
    428'.0076—dc21

                                                          2002004439

Printed in the United States of America
9 8 7 6 5 4 3 2
First Edition

ISBN 1-57685-423-X

For more information or to place an order, contact LearningExpress at:
    900 Broadway
    Suite 604
    New York, NY 10003

Or visit us at:
    www.learnatest.com

The LearningExpress Skill Builder in Focus Writing Team is comprised of experts in test preparation, as well as educators and teachers who specialize in language arts and math.

LearningExpress Skill Builder in Focus Writing Team

Brigit Dermott
Freelance Writer
English Tutor, New York Cares
New York, New York

Sandy Gade
Project Editor
LearningExpress
New York, New York

Kerry McLean
Project Editor
Math Tutor
Shirley, New York

William Recco
Middle School Math Teacher, Grade 8
New York Shoreham/Wading River School District
Math Tutor
St. James, New York

Colleen Schultz
Middle School Math Teacher, Grade 8
Vestal Central School District
Math Tutor
Vestal, New York

Contents

Introduction

Welcome to 501 Synonym and Antonym Questions! This book is designed to help you prepare for the verbal sections of many assessment and entrance exams. By completing the exercises in this book you will also increase your vocabulary and refine your knowledge of words.

Most standardized tests—including high school entrance exams, the SAT, civil service exams, and the GRE—use synonym and antonym questions to test verbal skills. These questions ask test takers to identify the word that is most similar or dissimilar to another word, effectively testing their knowledge of two words.

The questions in this book, for the most part, are grouped into sections of questions that ask you to select a word's synonym and sections that ask you to select a word's antonym. There are two sections that include questions asking for either the synonym or the antonym.

The questions increase in difficulty as you move through the exercises of each chapter. Because this book is designed for many levels of test takers, you may find that some of the more advanced questions are beyond your ability. If you are using this book to study for a high school entrance exam, you may get a number of questions that appear later in a section wrong. Don't worry! If you are getting the earlier questions correct, you are probably in good shape for your test. However, if you are studying for a graduate level exam such as the GRE, the full range of questions presented is appropriate for your level.

The questions in this book can help you prepare for your test in many ways. First, completing these practice exercises will make you familiar with the question format. They will also get you thinking of words in terms of other words with similar or opposite meanings. In the test-taking environment it can be difficult to switch gears from synonym questions to antonym questions; completing these exercises will make these mental gymnastics more comfortable.

Second, your performance on these questions will help you assess your vocabulary level. For example, a word may be familiar to you—you may have seen it in print and have a general sense of what it means—but when tested, you may discover that you do not know the word's precise meaning. These exercises will help you pinpoint those familiar words for which you need to learn the exact definition. In addition, you will probably encounter words that are totally unfamiliar. By memorizing their definitions, you can add these words to your vocabulary and call upon them at test time to improve your score.

Third, many of the questions in this book, and on assessment exams, test your ability to discern nuance of meaning. The question may ask you to identify the synonym for a secondary definition of a common word—for example, "inclination or natural ability" is a secondary definition of the word "bent." Also, the direction for these exercises usually ask you to identify the word that is "*most* similar" or "*most* dissimilar" in meaning to the word in the question. This means that you may be asked to pick between degrees of meaning. For example, "atrocious" means "utterly revolting"; in this case, "revolting" would be a more accurate synonym than "unpleasant."

Each question is fully explained at the end of the chapter. The answer keys give you not only the right answer but also the definitions of the word in the question and the correct answer. Use your performance to create a study guide. For example, make a list of all the words that you missed and their definitions. Then study this list as a quick and concentrated method to improve your vocabulary. In some cases, you will also benefit from looking up the definitions of the words that you selected incorrectly to ensure that you know the precise meaning of these words. Then add these words to your study list as well.

You have already taken an important step toward improving your vocabulary and your score. You have shown your commitment by purchasing this book. Now all you need to do is to complete each 35 to 40 question exercise, study the answers, and watch your vocabulary increase. You can even work in pencil and do the exercises again to reinforce what you have learned. Good luck!

1

Synonyms

Which of these words is closest in meaning to the word provided?

1. remote
   a. automatic
   b. distant
   c. savage
   d. mean

2. detest
   a. argue
   b. hate
   c. discover
   d. reveal

3. gracious
   a. pretty
   b. clever
   c. pleasant
   d. present

4. predict
   a. foretell
   b. decide
   c. prevent
   d. discover

5. kin
   a. exult
   b. twist
   c. friend
   d. relative

6. pensive
   a. oppressed
   b. caged
   c. thoughtful
   d. happy

7. banish
   a. exile
   b. hate
   c. fade
   d. clean

8. fraud
   a. malcontent
   b. argument
   c. imposter
   d. clown

9. saccharine
   a. leave
   b. sweet
   c. arid
   d. quit

10. drag
   a. sleepy
   b. crush
   c. proud
   d. pull

11. jovial
   a. incredulous
   b. merry
   c. revolting
   d. dizzy

12. indifferent
   a. neutral
   b. unkind
   c. precious
   d. mean

13. simulate
   a. excite
   b. imitate
   c. trick
   d. apelike

14. charisma
   a. ghost
   b. force
   c. charm
   d. courage

15. apportion
   a. divide
   b. decide
   c. cut
   d. squabble

16. generic
   a. general
   b. cheap
   c. fresh
   d. elderly

17. qualm
   a. distress
   b. impunity
   c. persevere
   d. scruple

18. wary
   a. calm
   b. curved
   c. confused
   d. cautious

19. distort
  a. wrong
  b. evil
  c. deform
  d. harm

20. sumptuous
  a. delirious
  b. gorgeous
  c. perilous
  d. luxurious

21. reel
  a. whirl
  b. fish
  c. hit
  d. mistake

22. inscrutable
  a. difficult
  b. mysterious
  c. inflexible
  d. wary

23. appall
  a. delirious
  b. covered
  c. dismay
  d. confuse

24. upright
  a. honorable
  b. horizontal
  c. humble
  d. supine

25. reverie
  a. palimpsest
  b. phantom
  c. daydream
  d. curio

26. loot
  a. destruction
  b. waste
  c. spoils
  d. cavort

27. loquacious
  a. talkative
  b. thirsty
  c. beautiful
  d. complicated

28. chimera
  a. chimney
  b. protest
  c. illusion
  d. panache

29. temerity
  a. audacity
  b. fearfulness
  c. shyness
  d. stupidity

30. educe
  a. demand
  b. elicit
  c. ideal
  d. unlawful

31. nabob
   a. bigwig
   b. doubter
   c. frolic
   d. converse

32. pall
   a. light
   b. satiate
   c. carry
   d. horror

33. sacrosanct
   a. prayer
   b. sanctuary
   c. pious
   d. sacred

34. louche
   a. gauche
   b. fine
   c. brilliant
   d. indecent

35. stentorian
   a. violent
   b. misbegotten
   c. loud
   d. stealthy

Answers

1. **b.** remote means faraway, or **distant**

2. **b.** to detest means to feel intense or violent dislike, or to **hate**

3. **c.** gracious means to be **pleasant** or considerate in social interactions

4. **a.** to predict means to declare in advance or to **foretell**

5. **d.** kin means people with common ancestors, or **relative**s

6. **c.** pensive means moodily or dreamily **thoughtful**

7. **a.** to banish means to drive out from home or country, or to **exile**

8. **c.** a fraud is someone who is not what he or she pretends to be, or an **imposter**

9. **b.** saccharine means overly **sweet**

10. **d.** to drag is to **pull**, or to cause movement in a direction with applied force

11. **b.** jovial means good humored or **merry**

12. **a.** to be indifferent is to be marked by impartiality or to be **neutral**

13. **b.** to simulate is to assume the outward appearance of, or to **imitate**

14. **c.** charisma is magnetic **charm** or appeal

15. **a.** to apportion is to **divide** and share out

16. **a.** generic means having the characteristic of a whole group, or **general**

17. **d.** a qualm is a feeling of uneasiness about a moral issue, or a **scruple**

18. **d.** wary means to be attentive especially to danger, or to be **cautious**

19. **c.** to distort means to twist out of a normal state, or to **deform**

20. **d.** sumptuous means excessively costly, rich, or **luxurious**

21. **a.** one meaning of reel is to move round and round, or to **whirl**

22. **b.** inscrutable means not easily interpreted or understood, or **mysterious**

23. **c.** to appall is to overcome with shock, or to **dismay**

24. **a.** upright can mean either **honorable** or vertical; horizontal and supine are both antonyms of upright

25. **c.** a reverie means the state of being lost in thought, or a **daydream**

26. **c.** loot means goods seized in war, or **spoils**

27. **a.** loquacious means excessively **talkative**, or garrulous

28. **c.** a chimera is a fabrication of the mind, or an **illusion**

29. **a.** temerity means unreasonable contempt for danger or recklessness, or **audacity**

30. **b.** to educe means to develop something potential or latent; to **elicit** means to draw out something hidden or latent

31. **a.** a nabob is a person of great wealth or importance, or a **bigwig**

32. **b.** to pall can mean to deprive of pleasure in something by **satiating**

33. d. sacrosanct means the most **sacred**, or holy

34. d. louche means not reputable, or **indecent**

35. c. stentorian means **loud** and is usually used to imply a voice of great power and range

2

Antonyms

Which of these words is most nearly the opposite of the word provided?

36. withdraw
   a. reduce
   b. need
   c. advance
   d. want

37. secret
   a. friendly
   b. covert
   c. hidden
   d. overt

38. heartfelt
   a. loving
   b. insincere
   c. unhealthy
   d. humorous

39. impartial
   a. hostile
   b. biased
   c. dislike
   d. worried

40. luminous
   a. clear
   b. dim
   c. brittle
   d. clever

41. awe
   a. borrow
   b. shallow
   c. low
   d. contempt

42. pit
  a. group
  b. peak
  c. select
  d. marry

43. rotund
  a. round
  b. unimportant
  c. thin
  d. dull

44. talent
  a. ungrateful
  b. silent
  c. show
  d. inability

45. common
  a. strange
  b. uneasy
  c. quick
  d. fast

46. brazen
  a. bashful
  b. boisterous
  c. noisy
  d. heated

47. expect
  a. attend
  b. regret
  c. despair
  d. loathe

48. malodorous
  a. acrid
  b. pungent
  c. fragrant
  d. delicious

49. expound
  a. besmirch
  b. confuse
  c. confine
  d. condemn

50. pique
  a. value
  b. gully
  c. smooth
  d. soothe

51. abate
  a. free
  b. augment
  c. provoke
  d. wane

52. dearth
  a. lack
  b. poverty
  c. abundance
  d. foreign

53. peaked
  a. tired
  b. arrogant
  c. pointy
  d. ruddy

54. abridge
  a. shorten
  b. extend
  c. stress
  d. easy

55. kindle
  a. smother
  b. detest
  c. enemy
  d. discourage

56. meager
  a. kind
  b. generous
  c. thoughtful
  d. copious

57. philistine
  a. novice
  b. intellectual
  c. pious
  d. debutante

58. zenith
  a. worst
  b. apex
  c. nadir
  d. past

59. germane
  a. irrelevant
  b. indifferent
  c. impartial
  d. improvident

60. irascible
  a. determined
  b. placid
  c. reasonable
  d. pliant

61. approbate
  a. ingratitude
  b. condemn
  c. dissatisfaction
  d. master

62. supercilious
  a. unimportant
  b. relevant
  c. serious
  d. meek

63. improvident
  a. cautious
  b. fortunate
  c. proven
  d. intelligent

64. demur
  a. embrace
  b. crude
  c. boisterous
  d. falter

65. fatuous
  a. crafty
  b. frugal
  c. sensible
  d. inane

66. quiescent
   a. lackadaisical
   b. active
   c. dull
   d. prescient

67. sartorial
   a. cheerful
   b. sincere
   c. inelegant
   d. homespun

68. sapient
   a. hunched
   b. strong
   c. simple
   d. simian

69. matutinal
   a. paternal
   b. crepuscular
   c. maritime
   d. marsupial

70. impecunious
   a. wealthy
   b. cautious
   c. hungry
   d. tardy

Answers

36. c. to withdraw means to remove or retreat; to **advance** is the opposite of retreat

37. d. secret means hidden or covert; **overt** means open to view

38. b. heartfelt means expressing genuine feeling, or sincere, so **insincere** is its opposite

39. b. impartial means to be without prejudice or bias, therefore **biased** is the opposite

40. b. luminous means radiating or reflecting light, or glowing; **dim** means dark or dull

41. d. awe means a sense of deep respect or veneration; **contempt** means a lack of respect, or disdain

42. b. a pit is a hole and a **peak** is the top of a hill or mountain

43. c. rotund means rounded or plump, therefore **thin** is the opposite

44. d. a talent is a special creative or artistic ability, therefore **inability** is the opposite

45. a. common means ordinary or familiar; **strange** means unfamiliar

46. a. brazen means to be defiant or insolent; **bashful** means to be shy or timid

47. c. to expect is to wait for or to look forward to; to **despair** is to lose all hope

48. c. malodorous means to have a bad smell; **fragrant** means smelling sweet or delicate

49. b. to expound means to explain; to **confuse**, or confound, is the opposite of expound

50. d. to pique means to excite or irritate; to **soothe** means to calm

51. b. to abate means to reduce in degree or intensity; to **augment** means to increase

52. c. dearth means an inadequate supply or lack of something; **abundance** means an ample quantity, or wealth

53. d. to be peaked is to appear pale or wan; to be **ruddy** is to have a healthy, red complexion

54. b. to abridge means to shorten and to **extend** means to lengthen

55. a. to kindle means to start burning or ignite; to **smother** means to stifle or suppress

56. d. meager means lacking in quality or quantity; **copious** means present in large quantity, or abundant

57. b. philistine is used disparagingly to describe a person guided by material rather than intellectual values; an **intellectual** is a person who engages in creative use of his or her intellect

58. a. zenith means the highest point or the apex; **nadir** means the lowest point

59. a. germane means to be appropriate or relevant, therefore **irrelevant** is the opposite

60. b. irascible means easily angered; **placid** means calm or serene

61. b. to approbate means to approve or sanction; to **condemn** means to declare wrong or to convict

62. d. supercilious means coolly or patronizingly haughty; **meek** means enduring injury with patience and without resentment

63. a. improvident means lacking prudent foresight, or careless; **cautious** means to be wary or to exercise forethought

64. a. to demur means to delay or hesitate; to **embrace** means to accept readily or gladly; demure means coy

65. c. fatuous means inanely foolish; **sensible** is its nearest opposite

66. b. quiescent means marked by inactivity or repose, therefore **active** is the opposite

67. a. sartorial means of or relating to tailored clothes; **homespun** means homemade

68. c. sapient means possessing great wisdom, or sage; one meaning of **simple** is deficient in intelligence

69. b. matutinal means of or relating to the morning; **crepuscular** means relating to or resembling twilight

70. a. impecunious means having little or no money, therefore **wealthy** is the opposite

3

Synonyms

Select the word that most nearly means the word provided.

71. modest most nearly means
   a. attractive
   b. clever
   c. current
   d. humble

72. custom most nearly means
   a. dessert
   b. habit
   c. ethic
   d. deliver

73. prolong most nearly means
   a. extend
   b. inquire
   c. relax
   d. wait

74. hustle most nearly means
   a. dance
   b. hurry
   c. busy
   d. clean

75. solemn most nearly means
   a. amusing
   b. harmful
   c. speech
   d. serious

76. imply most nearly means
   a. suggest
   b. stab
   c. thick
   d. destroy

77. ramble most nearly means
    a. knot
    b. confuse
    c. wander
    d. wonder

78. beneficial most nearly means
    a. help
    b. advantageous
    c. charity
    d. wise

79. flare most nearly means
    a. judicial
    b. temper
    c. style
    d. blaze

80. negligent most nearly means
    a. pajamas
    b. morbid
    c. careless
    d. dark

81. aloof most nearly means
    a. above
    b. tidy
    c. clever
    d. reserved

82. resolve most nearly means
    a. turn
    b. puzzle
    c. decide
    d. want

83. congregate most nearly means
    a. worship
    b. gather
    c. disturb
    d. hurry

84. utter most nearly means
    a. express
    b. defer
    c. borrow
    d. laugh

85. fearless most nearly means
    a. powerful
    b. cowardly
    c. brave
    d. careful

86. negligible most nearly means
    a. insignificant
    b. arguable
    c. careless
    d. dark

87. placid most nearly means
    a. calm
    b. lazy
    c. solemn
    d. devious

88. rake most nearly means
    a. thin
    b. scoundrel
    c. gentleman
    d. shovel

89. dupe most nearly means
   a. rancher
   b. trick
   c. simpleton
   d. drug

90. stigma most nearly means
   a. stain
   b. trial
   c. difficulty
   d. holiness

91. reside most nearly means
   a. remain
   b. home
   c. dwell
   d. sediment

92. covetous most nearly means
   a. quiet
   b. sneaky
   c. lurking
   d. greedy

93. abide most nearly means
   a. endure
   b. hate
   c. attendance
   d. live

94. shrewd most nearly means
   a. intractable
   b. mean
   c. astute
   d. intelligent

95. fetter most nearly means
   a. rancid
   b. praise
   c. hamper
   d. persist

96. flagrant most nearly means
   a. vibrant
   b. glaring
   c. vicious
   d. pleasant

97. mitigate most nearly means
   a. relieve
   b. blend
   c. defend
   d. confuse

98. rail most nearly means
   a. scold
   b. push
   c. try
   d. punish

99. meld most nearly means
   a. character
   b. distinction
   c. blend
   d. firmness

100. rally most nearly means
   a. demonstrate
   b. muster
   c. course
   d. truly

101. abject most nearly means
a. indigent
b. desire
c. despondent
d. extreme

102. bespoke most nearly means
a. gentle
b. quiet
c. tailored
d. handsome

103. diffident most nearly means
a. apathetic
b. shy
c. arrogant
d. quarrelsome

104. proffer most nearly means
a. mendicant
b. wastrel
c. predict
d. tender

105. mordant most nearly means
a. dead
b. gruesome
c. fetid
d. caustic

106. churlish most nearly means
a. childish
b. boorish
c. tempestuous
d. disorderly

107. antediluvian most nearly means
a. antiquated
b. parched
c. nonsectarian
d. nonsensical

108. picayune most nearly means
a. petty
b. spicy
c. paltry
d. southern

109. smite most nearly means
a. flee
b. speck
c. dirt
d. strike

110. winnow most nearly means
a. carve
b. wind
c. weed
d. carry

Answers

71. **d.** modest means to be free of conceit or pretension, or **humble**

72. **b.** a custom means a long-established practice, or a **habit**

73. **a.** to prolong means to lengthen in time, or to **extend**

74. **b.** to hustle means to **hurry**

75. **d.** solemn means marked by grave sobriety, or **serious**

76. **a.** to imply means to express indirectly, or to **suggest**

77. **c.** to ramble means to move aimlessly from place to place, or to **wander**

78. **b.** beneficial means causing benefit, or **advantageous**

79. **d.** flare means a fire or **blaze** used to signal; flair means talent or style

80. **c.** negligent means marked by neglect, or **careless**

81. **d.** aloof means distant in feeling, or **reserved**

82. **c.** one meaning of resolve is to **decide**, often to stop from doing something

83. **b.** to congregate means to **gather** in a group

84. **a.** to utter means to **express** in words

85. **c.** fearless means lacking fear, or **brave**

86. **a.** negligible means so small or **insignificant** as to deserve little attention

87. **a.** placid means free of disturbance, or **calm**

88. **b.** a rake is a dissolute person, or a **scoundrel**

89. **b.** to dupe means to deceive or to **trick**

90. **a.** stigma means a mark of shame or discredit, or a **stain**

91. **c.** to reside means to occupy a place as one's home, or to **dwell**

92. **d.** covetous means having an inordinate desire for wealth, or **greedy**

93. **a.** to abide means to **endure** without yielding, or to withstand

94. **c.** shrewd means marked by clever awareness, or **astute**

95. **c.** to fetter means to **hamper**, or to restrain

96. **b.** flagrant means obviously wrong or immoral; **glaring** means painfully obvious

97. **a.** mitigate means to make less severe or painful, or to **relieve**

98. **a.** to rail means to **scold** in harsh, abusive language

99. **c.** to meld means to merge or to **blend**

100. **b.** to rally means to arouse for action, or to **muster**

101. **c.** abject means cast down in spirit, or utterly hopeless; **despondent** means having lost all hope

102. **c.** bespoke means custom-made; **tailored** also means custom-made

103. **b.** diffident means **shy** or lacking in confidence

104. **d.** to proffer means to put something forward for acceptance, or to **tender**

105. **d.** mordant means biting or **caustic** in means or speech

106. **b.** churlish means resembling an ill-bred or vulgar person, or **boorish**

107. **a.** antediluvian means so ancient that it could have come before the time of the flood and Noah's ark, or **antiquated**

108. **c.** picayune means trivial or of little value; **paltry** means trivial or meager

109. **d.** smite means to **strike** heavily especially with the hand

110. **c.** to winnow means to sift or get rid of, like **weed**, it is often used with "out"

4

Antonyms

Select the word that is most opposite to the word provided.

111. detain is most opposite to
    a. release
    b. silence
    c. forget
    d. prosper

112. famous is most opposite to
    a. boring
    b. poor
    c. obscure
    d. untalented

113. colossal is most opposite to
    a. easy
    b. tiny
    c. graceful
    d. roof

114. fluid is most opposite to
    a. solid
    b. liquid
    c. afraid
    d. decent

115. continue is most opposite to
    a. curve
    b. argue
    c. carry
    d. pause

116. labor is most opposite to
    a. amuse
    b. cat
    c. rest
    d. strive

117. brawny is most opposite to
    a. swift
    b. weak
    c. strong
    d. pale

118. fickle is most opposite to
    a. steady
    b. kind
    c. please
    d. finagle

119. inept is most opposite to
    a. clumsy
    b. infer
    c. competent
    d. foolish

120. pivotal is most opposite to
    a. turning
    b. wavy
    c. unimportant
    d. clear

121. cursed is most opposite to
    a. swore
    b. pious
    c. unfortunate
    d. lucky

122. candid is most opposite to
    a. unkind
    b. blunt
    c. valid
    d. dishonest

123. flaunt is most opposite to
    a. regard
    b. sink
    c. hide
    d. propose

124. heal is most opposite to
    a. sew
    b. foot
    c. good
    d. maim

125. pacify is most opposite to
    a. excite
    b. land
    c. coddle
    d. unhand

126. sullen is most opposite to
    a. dirty
    b. cheerful
    c. clean
    d. risen

127. assure is most opposite to
    a. alarm
    b. reassure
    c. quiet
    d. unsure

128. fallacious is most opposite to
    a. perfect
    b. truthful
    c. accidental
    d. disarming

129. gumption is most opposite to
  a. seriousness
  b. apathy
  c. levity
  d. despair

130. ecstasy is most opposite to
  a. hate
  b. agony
  c. languor
  d. fatigue

131. astute is most opposite to
  a. distraught
  b. careful
  c. generous
  d. gullible

132. winsome is most opposite to
  a. dour
  b. attractive
  c. mysterious
  d. clever

133. droll is most opposite to
  a. forget
  b. charm
  c. sedate
  d. absurd

134. enigmatic is most opposite to
  a. healthy
  b. watchful
  c. disastrous
  d. obvious

135. obtuse is most opposite to
  a. slim
  b. acute
  c. opaque
  d. thick

136. obsequious is most opposite to
  a. clear
  b. clever
  c. domineering
  d. dandified

137. doleful is most opposite to
  a. empty
  b. rich
  c. witty
  d. vivacious

138. wanton is most opposite to
  a. merciful
  b. repast
  c. brilliant
  d. vicious

139. banal is most opposite to
  a. sincere
  b. wealthy
  c. extraordinary
  d. trustworthy

140. lugubrious is most opposite to
  a. quick
  b. cheerful
  c. salubrious
  d. dry

141. perspicacious is most opposite to
  a. calm
  b. easy
  c. dull
  d. winsome

142. elan is most opposite to
  a. inelegance
  b. stupidity
  c. obscure
  d. despair

143. recondite is most opposite to
  a. manifest
  b. flexible
  c. provident
  d. sociable

144. gainsay is most opposite to
  a. regret
  b. own
  c. prudent
  d. prude

145. effluvium is most opposite to
  a. land
  b. essential
  c. fragrance
  d. solid

146. parsimony is most opposite to
  a. generosity
  b. sinfulness
  c. verbosity
  d. tenderness

147. truculent is most opposite to
  a. faltering
  b. gentle
  c. facile
  d. submissive

148. spurious is most opposite to
  a. disingenuous
  b. thoughtless
  c. placid
  d. genuine

149. welter is most opposite to
  a. order
  b. freeze
  c. patron
  d. sustain

150. eclat is most opposite to
  a. apathy
  b. dullness
  c. silence
  d. disinterest

Answers

111. **a.** to detain means to hold or keep back; to **release** means to let go

112. **c.** famous means widely known; **obscure** means little known

113. **b.** colossal means incredibly large, therefore **tiny** is the opposite

114. **a.** a fluid is a substance that flows; a **solid** does not flow

115. **d.** to continue means to act without interruption; to **pause** means to stop temporarily

116. **c.** to labor means to work; to **rest** means to cease working

117. **b.** brawny means muscled or strong, therefore **weak** is the opposite

118. **a.** fickle means to lack steadiness, therefore **steady** is the opposite

119. **c.** inept means to lack competence, therefore **competent** is the opposite

120. **c.** pivotal means very important, or crucial, therefore **unimportant** is the opposite

121. **d.** cursed means to be the subject of misfortune, or to be unlucky, therefore **lucky** is the opposite

122. **d.** candid means to be frank, or honest, therefore **dishonest** is the opposite

123. **c.** to flaunt means to display showily, or to show off, therefore **hide** is the opposite

124. **d.** to heal means to restore to health; to **maim** means to injure

125. **a.** to pacify means to soothe, or calm, therefore **excite** is the opposite

126. **b.** sullen means showing a disagreeable mood, or lacking cheer, therefore **cheerful** is the opposite

127. **a.** to assure means to make sure by removing doubt or worry; **alarm** means to give warning or to arouse fear

128. **b.** fallacious means tending to deceive; **truthful** means disposed to tell the truth

129. **b.** gumption means initiative, or drive; **apathy** means a lack of interest or concern

130. **b.** ecstasy means a state of rapturous delight; **agony** means intense pain of mind or body

131. **d.** astute means shrewd or showing acute mental vision; **gullible** means easily duped or cheated

132. **a.** winsome means cheerful and engaging; **dour** means gloomy or sullen

133. **c.** droll means to have a humorous or odd quality; **sedate** means unruffled or serious

134. **d.** enigmatic means mysterious or obscure, therefore **obvious** is the opposite

135. **b.** obtuse means insensitive or stupid; **acute** means marked by keen perception or shrewd

136. **c.** obsequious means subservient or fawning; **domineering** means exercising overbearing control

137. **d.** doleful means full of grief or cheerless; **vivacious** means full of life and spirit

138. **a.** one meaning of wanton is malicious or merciless, therefore **merciful** is the opposite

139. **c.** banal means trite or commonplace, therefore **extraordinary** is the opposite

140. **b.** lugubrious means mournful, or dismal, therefore **cheerful** is the opposite

141. **c.** perspicacious means keen or astute, therefore **dull** is the opposite

142. **d.** elan means vigorous spirit or enthusiasm; **despair** means an utter loss of hope

143. **a.** recondite means difficult for one of ordinary understanding to comprehend; **manifest** means easily understood or recognized

144. **b.** to gainsay means to deny; one meaning of to **own** is to admit

145. **c.** effluvium means an offensive smell; **fragrance** means a sweet or delicate odor

146. **a.** parsimony means thrift or stinginess, therefore **generosity** is the opposite

147. **b.** truculent means cruel or savage, therefore **gentle** is the opposite

148. **d.** spurious means lacking genuine qualities, or false, therefore **genuine** is the opposite

149. **a.** welter means a state of wild disorder, or turmoil, therefore **order** is the opposite

150. **b.** eclat means a dazzling effect, or brilliance, therefore **dullness** is the opposite

5

Synonyms

Which of these words most nearly means the word provided?

151. deplete
   a. decorate
   b. beg
   c. exhaust
   d. hurry

152. voluntary
   a. willing
   b. charity
   c. prisoner
   d. careless

153. refute
   a. garbage
   b. deny
   c. offer
   d. difficult

154. cheat
   a. stingy
   b. argue
   c. freckle
   d. defraud

155. miserable
   a. cruel
   b. wrong
   c. unhappy
   d. miss

156. vintage
   a. classic
   b. alcoholic
   c. disease
   d. spoiled

157. tart
  a. law
  b. acid
  c. angry
  d. desirable

158. corner
  a. display
  b. trap
  c. paint
  d. hurry

159. zest
  a. gusto
  b. cram
  c. worry
  d. trial

160. haggle
  a. tired
  b. climb
  c. decrease
  d. bargain

161. impel
  a. force
  b. block
  c. hinder
  d. discredit

162. throng
  a. garment
  b. bell
  c. mass
  d. weight

163. imperial
  a. bratty
  b. oppressive
  c. regal
  d. beautiful

164. diffuse
  a. difficult
  b. scatter
  c. incomprehensible
  d. unplug

165. hinder
  a. lose
  b. loose
  c. despair
  d. check

166. latent
  a. dormant
  b. recent
  c. effeminate
  d. desirable

167. wretched
  a. twisted
  b. forced
  c. miserable
  d. increased

168. irksome
  a. outrageous
  b. fearsome
  c. impoverished
  d. annoying

169. regulate
  a. even
  b. police
  c. flow
  d. position

170. warrant
  a. justify
  b. burrow
  c. hide
  d. integrity

171. protract
  a. hire
  b. fold
  c. delay
  d. corner

172. lax
  a. ensure
  b. slack
  c. servant
  d. strive

173. rigor
  a. austerity
  b. rope
  c. fix
  d. excess

174. discrete
  a. leave
  b. diminish
  c. squander
  d. distinct

175. lissome
  a. slow
  b. honest
  c. supple
  d. dull

176. misprize
  a. despise
  b. devalue
  c. erroneous
  d. covet

177. impugn
  a. imply
  b. fret
  c. assail
  d. recalcitrant

178. supervene
  a. intervene
  b. overreach
  c. displace
  d. follow

179. exigent
  a. urgent
  b. treatise
  c. miser
  d. expedient

180. fervid
  a. delightful
  b. difficult
  c. obstinate
  d. ardent

181. ersatz
  a. chaotic
  b. artificial
  c. impromptu
  d. vague

182. redolent
  a. ubiquitous
  b. odorous
  c. shy
  d. bellicose

183. turpitude
  a. lethargy
  b. honor
  c. belligerence
  d. depravity

184. propinquity
  a. habit
  b. nearness
  c. capacity
  d. tendency

185. vociferous
  a. numerous
  b. bountiful
  c. strident
  d. garrulous

Answers

151. c. deplete means to reduce or deprive or something essential; **exhaust** means to empty completely

152. a. voluntary means done by one's own will, or **willing**

153. b. to refute means to prove wrong, or to **deny** the truth of

154. d. to cheat means to influence by means of trickery, or to **defraud**

155. c. miserable means in a state of distress or **unhappiness**

156. a. vintage means of old and enduring interest, or **classic**

157. b. tart means pleasantly sharp or **acid** to the taste

158. b. to corner means to drive into a corner, or to **trap**

159. a. one meaning of zest is keen enjoyment, or **gusto**

160. d. to haggle means to negotiate over terms or price, or to **bargain**

161. a. to impel means to drive forward using strong moral pressure, or to **force**

162. c. a throng is a large number of assembled people, or a **mass**

163. c. imperial means befitting or suggesting an emperor; **regal** means befitting or suggesting a king

164. b. to diffuse means to break up or spread out, or to **scatter**

165. **d.** to hinder means to hold back; one meaning of to **check** means to slow or bring to a stop

166. **a.** latent means capable of becoming but not currently visible, or **dormant**

167. **c.** wretched means extremely distressed, or **miserable**

168. **d.** irksome means tedious or **annoying**

169. **b.** to regulate means to bring under the control of law; to **police** means to control or keep order

170. **a.** to warrant means to serve as adequate ground or reason, or to **justify**

171. **c.** to protract means to prolong in time or space, or to **delay**

172. **b.** lax means in a relaxed state, or **slack**

173. **a.** rigor means severity of life, or **austerity**

174. **d.** discrete means individually **distinct**

175. **c.** lissome means **supple** or flexible

176. **a.** to misprize means to hold in contempt, or to **despise**

177. **c.** to impugn means to attack verbally as false or lacking integrity; to **assail** means to attack

178. **d.** to supervene means to **follow** as an unexpected development

179. **a.** exigent means demanding immediate attention, or **urgent**

180. **d.** fervid means **ardent** or passionate

181. **b.** ersatz means a usually **artificial** or inferior substitute

182. **b.** redolent means aromatic or full of a specific scent, or **odorous**

183. **d.** turpitude means wickedness, or **depravity**

184. **b.** propinquity means **nearness** in place or time

185. **c.** vociferous means loud and insistent, often in presentation of demands or requests; **strident** also means loud and insistent

Antonyms

Which word is most dissimilar in meaning to the word provided?

186. gracious
    a. cordial
    b. rude
    c. furious
    d. tactile

187. valor
    a. cowardice
    b. false
    c. drop
    d. heavy

188. severe
    a. lenient
    b. cautious
    c. join
    d. one

189. imaginative
    a. playful
    b. written
    c. small
    d. dull

190. knowing
    a. wasteful
    b. dense
    c. clumsy
    d. fast

191. animosity
    a. love
    b. plantlike
    c. barren
    d. tiny

192. exact
  a. join
  b. sympathetic
  c. incorrect
  d. whole

193. extravagant
  a. unknown
  b. homebody
  c. punctual
  d. moderate

194. stamina
  a. weakness
  b. clear
  c. decisive
  d. calmness

195. rough
  a. tumble
  b. sleek
  c. fast
  d. distant

196. garner
  a. unravel
  b. mar
  c. squander
  d. tarnish

197. prodigal
  a. thrifty
  b. secondary
  c. distant
  d. squalid

198. tacit
  a. grand
  b. dictated
  c. illicit
  d. messy

199. repudiate
  a. argue
  b. soften
  c. slander
  d. admit

200. pristine
  a. free
  b. sullied
  c. wide
  d. thorough

201. concede
  a. sit
  b. withstand
  c. dismiss
  d. elaborate

202. placate
  a. appease
  b. strip
  c. tremendous
  d. enrage

203. popular
  a. empty
  b. uncommon
  c. famous
  d. feisty

204. felicitous
   a. morbid
   b. boorish
   c. inopportune
   d. delightful

205. austere
   a. lavish
   b. unfavorable
   c. light
   d. devout

206. insipid
   a. cold
   b. brave
   c. exciting
   d. bashful

207. wastrel
   a. sober
   b. spendthrift
   c. mute
   d. miser

208. temperate
   a. Celsius
   b. inordinate
   c. lukewarm
   d. safely

209. nebulous
   a. cloudy
   b. dim
   c. distinct
   d. desirable

210. adroit
   a. clumsy
   b. left
   c. diplomatic
   d. unpersuasive

211. mite
   a. weakness
   b. tend
   c. bulk
   d. drive

212. supernal
   a. nocturnal
   b. special
   c. despicable
   d. hellish

213. reprobate
   a. sage
   b. elevated
   c. possess
   d. dismiss

214. specious
   a. genuine
   b. logical
   c. common
   d. deliberate

215. effete
   a. conquer
   b. proper
   c. prosperous
   d. civilized

216. rabble
 a. order
 b. clear
 c. open
 d. union

217. protean
 a. unformed
 b. unchanging
 c. elaborate
 d. selective

218. vertiginous
 a. horizontal
 b. litigious
 c. constant
 d. lowly

219. parvenu
 a. wallflower
 b. highway
 c. melody
 d. plan

220. lapidarian
 a. square
 b. secular
 c. pasture
 d. inelegant

Answers

186. **b.** gracious means to be pleasant in a social situation, or cordial; **rude** means to be unpleasant

187. **a.** valor means strength of mind or spirit, or courage; **cowardice** means lack of courage

188. **a.** one meaning of severe is strict; **lenient** means mild or indulgent

189. **d.** imaginative means having imagination; **dull** means lacking imagination

190. **b.** knowing means having information or knowledge; **dense** means dull or stupid

191. **a.** animosity means resentment or hostility, therefore **love** is the opposite

192. **c.** exact means in complete accordance with fact, or correct, therefore **incorrect** is the opposite

193. **d.** extravagant means lacking in restraint and moderation, therefore **moderate** is the opposite

194. **a.** stamina means strength or endurance, therefore **weakness** is the opposite

195. **b.** rough means having an uneven, coarse surface; **sleek** means having a smooth, bright surface

196. **c.** to garner means to gather or to store; to **squander** means to cause to disperse or to scatter

197. **a.** prodigal means wasteful or extravagant; **thrifty** means thriving by industry and frugality

198. **b.** tacit means unspoken, or implied; **dictated** means spoken

199. **d.** to repudiate means to reject or deny, therefore to **admit** is the opposite

200. **b.** pristine means unspoiled or pure; **sullied** means spoiled or tarnished

201. **b.** to concede means to yield; to **withstand** means to successfully resist

202. **d.** to placate means to soothe or calm; to **enrage** means to anger

203. **b.** popular means frequently encountered or accepted, or common, therefore **uncommon** is the opposite

204. **c.** felicitous means very well-suited or apt; **inopportune** means inconvenient or not well-suited

205. **a.** austere means simple and unadorned; **lavish** means produced or expended in abundance

206. **c.** insipid means lacking in qualities that interest or excite, therefore **exciting** is the opposite

207. **d.** a wastrel is someone who spends foolishly or self-indulgently; a **miser** is someone who hoards his or her wealth

208. **b.** temperate means moderate; **inordinate** means excessive or immoderate

209. **c.** nebulous means vague or indistinct, therefore **distinct** is the opposite

210. **a.** adroit means skillful in the use of the hands, therefore **clumsy** is the opposite

211. **c.** mite means a very small or insignificant part; **bulk** means the main or greater part

212. **d.** supernal means coming from on high, or heavenly; **infernal** is a synonym for hellish

213. **b.** reprobate means morally debased or depraved; one meaning of **elevated** is to be on a moral or intellectual high plane

214. **a.** specious means having a false look of truth or genuineness, therefore **genuine** is the opposite

215. **b.** effete means weak or decadent; one meaning of **proper** is virtuous or respectable

216. **d.** a rabble is a disorderly or disorganized crowd of people; a **union** is a group of individuals joined in an organized manner

217. **b.** protean means showing great diversity or variability, or versatile, therefore **unchanging** is the opposite

218. **c.** vertiginous means inclined to frequent change, or inconstant, therefore **constant** is the opposite

219. **a.** a parvenu is an upstart or a social climber; a **wallflower** is someone who refrains from socializing

220. **d.** lapidarian means having elegance or precision and comes from the word lapidary, which means a cutter or engraver of precious stones, therefore **inelegant** is the opposite

7

Synonyms and Antonyms

Read each question carefully and select the word that is most similar or dissimilar in meaning to the word provided.

221. delirious is most similar to
   a. manic
   b. calm
   c. tasty
   d. suspicious

222. infirm is most similar to
   a. hospital
   b. weak
   c. short
   d. fortitude

223. cautious is most dissimilar to
   a. reasonable
   b. careful
   c. illogical
   d. reckless

224. lure is most similar to
   a. tickle
   b. decoy
   c. resist
   d. suspect

225. perilous is most dissimilar to
   a. disciplined
   b. similar
   c. safe
   d. honest

226. isolation is most similar to
   a. fear
   b. plentitude
   c. solitude
   d. disease

227. lull is most similar to
  a. pause
  b. noise
  c. boring
  d. mark

228. outfit is most similar to
  a. indoors
  b. strong
  c. special
  d. furnish

229. punctual is most dissimilar to
  a. close
  b. tardy
  c. sloppy
  d. precious

230. delude is most dissimilar to
  a. drought
  b. clever
  c. enlighten
  d. enrage

231. omit is most similar to
  a. recluse
  b. neglect
  c. mistake
  d. destroy

232. resilient is most dissimilar to
  a. stubborn
  b. careless
  c. substantial
  d. flimsy

233. mutiny is most similar to
  a. rebellion
  b. currency
  c. sailor
  d. hassle

234. naive is most similar to
  a. rural
  b. secular
  c. unsophisticated
  d. sultry

235. entice is most dissimilar to
  a. piece
  b. repulse
  c. attract
  d. repeat

236. solemnity is most similar to
  a. lightheartedness
  b. gravity
  c. diligence
  d. sleepiness

237. stingy is most dissimilar to
  a. wasteful
  b. democratic
  c. spiteful
  d. liberal

238. malign is most similar to
  a. evil
  b. malicious
  c. slander
  d. grandiose

239. impudent is most similar to
   a. cautious
   b. haphazard
   c. gleeful
   d. insolent

240. vacillate is most dissimilar to
   a. decide
   b. teeter
   c. dilate
   d. please

241. kinetic is most dissimilar to
   a. cold
   b. static
   c. lewd
   d. foolish

242. lambaste is most similar to
   a. marinade
   b. commotion
   c. censure
   d. tickle

243. kowtow is most dissimilar to
   a. snub
   b. pull
   c. fawn
   d. forage

244. rudimentary is most similar to
   a. crass
   b. gracious
   c. deliberate
   d. primitive

245. pitched is most similar to
   a. undone
   b. retracted
   c. heated
   d. lovely

246. tepid is most dissimilar to
   a. dispassionate
   b. scalding
   c. crisp
   d. clever

247. largesse is most similar to
   a. greatness
   b. generosity
   c. miniscule
   d. clumsiness

248. insidious is most dissimilar to
   a. repellant
   b. pure
   c. charming
   d. delicious

249. decorum is most similar to
   a. etiquette
   b. merit
   c. parliament
   d. slipshod

250. succor is most dissimilar to
   a. genius
   b. abet
   c. injure
   d. deciduous

251. enjoin is most dissimilar to
a. sever
b. dislike
c. permit
d. divorce

252. tumid is most similar to
a. swollen
b. fetid
c. aggressive
d. despondent

253. jejune is most similar to
a. youthful
b. insipid
c. charming
d. quick

254. ecumenical is most dissimilar to
a. spiritual
b. humanistic
c. secular
d. parochial

255. sinecure is most similar to
a. cakewalk
b. serpentine
c. evil
d. dishonest

256. castigate is most similar to
a. neuter
b. punish
c. banish
d. celebrate

257. reconnoiter is most dissimilar to
a. disarm
b. disassemble
c. distance
d. disregard

258. obloquy is most similar to
a. tirade
b. dependence
c. oval
d. circumlocution

259. recondite is most dissimilar to
a. give
b. obscure
c. patent
d. hardy

260. querulous is most similar to
a. nauseous
b. fretful
c. curious
d. dizzy

Answers

221. **a.** delirious means marked by frenzied excitement, or **manic**

222. **b.** infirm means feeble from age, or **weak**

223. **d.** cautious means careful; **reckless** means lacking caution

224. **b.** a lure is used to attract animals into a trap, like a **decoy**

225. **c.** perilous means dangerous, therefore **safe** is the opposite

226. **c.** isolation means the state of being alone or withdrawn, or **solitude**

227. **a.** a lull is a temporary **pause**

228. **d.** to outfit means to supply or to **furnish**

229. **b.** punctual means on time; **tardy** means late

230. **c.** to delude means to mislead the judgment of someone, or to trick; to **enlighten** means to give knowledge to someone

231. **b.** to omit means to leave out, to fail to perform, or to **neglect**

232. **d.** resilient means capable of withstanding shock; **flimsy** means lacking in physical strength or substance

233. **a.** mutiny means resistance to lawful authority, or **rebellion**

234. **c.** naive means unaffectedly simple, or **unsophisticated**

235. **b.** to entice means attract seductively, or to lure; to **repulse** means to cause aversion to, or to disgust

236. **b.** solemnity means formal or ceremonious observance, or seriousness; **gravity** means dignity of bearing, or seriousness

237. **d.** one meaning of **liberal** is giving freely, or generous; stingy means lacking generosity

238. **c.** to malign means to speak false or harmful things of, or to **slander**

239. **d.** impudent means contemptuously bold or cocky, or **insolent**

240. **a.** vacillate means to hesitate among choices, or to waver; **decide** means to choose

241. **b.** kinetic means relating to motion, or dynamic; **static** means at rest, or stationary

242. **c.** to lambaste means to attack verbally, or to **censure**

243. **a.** to kowtow means to show fawning deference; to **snub** means to treat with contempt

244. **d.** rudimentary means crude or **primitive**

245. **c.** pitched means intensely fought; one meaning of **heated** is marked by anger

246. **b.** tepid means lukewarm; **scalding** means boiling hot

247. **b.** largesse means liberal giving or **generosity**

248. **a.** insidious means harmful but enticing or seductive; **repellant** means arousing aversion or disgust

249. **a.** decorum means conduct required in social life, or **etiquette**

250. **c.** to succor means go to the aid of, or relieve; to **injure** means to harm

251. **c.** enjoin means to forbid or prohibit, therefore **permit** is the opposite

252. **a.** tumid means puffy or **swollen**

253. **b.** jejune means lacking in substance or interest; **insipid** means lacking in qualities to excite or interest

254. **d.** ecumenical means of or relating to the whole body of churches, or universal; **parochial** means of or relating to a parish, or limited in scope or range

255. **a.** a sinecure is a job for which little or no work is expected; a **cakewalk** is a one-sided competition

256. **b.** to castigate means to subject to severe **punish**ment

257. **d.** reconnoiter means to gain information or to explore; **disregard** means to pay no attention to

258. **a.** obloquy means abusive language; **tirade** means harshly censorious language

259. **c.** recondite means hidden from sight or obscure; **patent** means readily visible or intelligible

260. **b.** querulous means habitually complaining, or **fretful**

8

Synonyms

Select the word that is most similar in meaning to the word provided.

261. wrath
 a. knot
 b. anger
 c. crime
 d. smoke

262. plethora
 a. trouble
 b. foolish
 c. wealth
 d. love

263. calamity
 a. potion
 b. silence
 c. shellfish
 d. disaster

264. pompous
 a. arrogant
 b. supportive
 c. busy
 d. gaudy

265. prevalent
 a. wind
 b. servile
 c. widespread
 d. rare

266. wince
 a. flinch
 b. cheer
 c. crush
 d. solitary

267. superficial
   a. gorgeous
   b. shallow
   c. intelligent
   d. rich

268. tangle
   a. snarl
   b. growl
   c. dance
   d. shiver

269. reform
   a. punish
   b. destroy
   c. display
   d. correct

270. methodical
   a. rhythmic
   b. poetic
   c. systematic
   d. disrespectful

271. spite
   a. joy
   b. beverage
   c. wonder
   d. malice

272. scale
   a. climb
   b. sail
   c. swim
   d. skate

273. smudge
   a. gloat
   b. residue
   c. blur
   d. celebrate

274. drizzle
   a. curly
   b. sprinkle
   c. sear
   d. drench

275. mundane
   a. dirty
   b. commonplace
   c. confused
   d. extraordinary

276. pretension
   a. stress
   b. ambition
   c. waste
   d. strife

277. affect
   a. outcome
   b. share
   c. pompous
   d. cultivate

278. herald
   a. insignia
   b. postpone
   c. hail
   d. regal

279. faculty
  a. defective
  b. school
  c. gift
  d. desire

280. mirth
  a. anger
  b. glee
  c. sarcasm
  d. mistrust

281. drudgery
  a. silliness
  b. labor
  c. evil
  d. investigation

282. prerequisite
  a. necessary
  b. course
  c. difficult
  d. tar

283. dire
  a. questionable
  b. forthright
  c. traitor
  d. urgent

284. grapple
  a. struggle
  b. trap
  c. laugh
  d. intend

285. sundry
  a. aged
  b. supply
  c. various
  d. tremendous

286. supplant
  a. grow
  b. replace
  c. undo
  d. question

287. venerate
  a. ordain
  b. breathe
  c. polish
  d. revere

288. conciliate
  a. appease
  b. disagree
  c. revive
  d. separate

289. exultant
  a. afraid
  b. jubilant
  c. expectant
  d. demanding

290. surreptitious
  a. overbearing
  b. clandestine
  c. indirect
  d. impious

291. recalcitrant
   a. hesitant
   b. subdued
   c. unruly
   d. subtract

292. pretty
   a. plain
   b. confusing
   c. ugly
   d. terrible

293. coterie
   a. various
   b. flirtation
   c. club
   d. socialize

294. nefarious
   a. infamous
   b. macabre
   c. evil
   d. distinguished

295. curry
   a. flatter
   b. spicy
   c. squander
   d. game

296. preternatural
   a. immature
   b. extraordinary
   c. removed
   d. unearned

297. pernicious
   a. noxious
   b. illicit
   c. open
   d. undecided

298. reprisal
   a. accusation
   b. loathe
   c. retaliation
   d. insinuation

299. manifold
   a. evident
   b. contemporary
   c. diverse
   d. willing

300. factious
   a. sham
   b. unreliable
   c. seditious
   d. argumentative

Answers

261. **b.** wrath means strong, vengeful **anger**

262. **c.** abundance means an ample quantity, or **wealth**

263. **d.** a calamity is an extraordinarily grave event, or **disaster**

264. **a.** pompous means self-important, or **arrogant**

265. **c.** prevalent means generally accepted, or **widespread**

266. **a.** to wince means to shrink back involuntarily, or to **flinch**

267. **b.** superficial means to be concerned only with the surface or appearance, or **shallow**

268. **a.** a tangle is a twisted, knotted mass, or a **snarl**

269. **d.** to reform means to change for the better, or to **correct**

270. **c.** methodical means proceeding according to an order or system, or **systematic**

271. **d.** spite means petty ill will or hatred, or **malice**

272. **a.** one meaning of scale is to **climb**

273. **c.** a smudge is a **blur**ry spot or streak

274. **b.** one meaning of to drizzle is to rain in very small drops, or to **sprinkle**

275. **b.** mundane means ordinary, or **commonplace**

276. **b.** pretension means an effort to establish, or **ambition**

277. **d.** to affect means to make a display of using or liking something, or to **cultivate**

278. **c.** to herald means to greet with enthusiasm, or to **hail**

279. **c.** one meaning of faculty is an ability or **gift**

280. **b.** mirth means gladness expressed with laughter, or **glee**

281. **b.** drudgery means uninspiring or menial **labor**

282. **a.** prerequisite means **necessary** for carrying out a function

283. **d.** dire means desperately **urgent**

284. **a.** to grapple means to come to grips with, or to **struggle**

285. **c.** sundry means an indeterminate number, or **various**

286. **b.** to supplant means take the place of, or to **replace**

287. **d.** to venerate means to treat with reverential respect, or to **revere**

288. **a.** to conciliate means to gain goodwill with pleasing acts, or to **appease**

289. **b.** exultant means filled with or expressing great joy, or **jubilant**

290. **b.** surreptitious means done or acquired in stealth, or **clandestine**

291. **c.** recalcitrant means defiant of authority, or **unruly**

292. **d.** one meaning of pretty is miserable or **terrible**, as in the expression "a pretty pickle"

293. **c.** a coterie is an intimate or exclusive group or people who share a common interest or purpose; a **club** is an association of people for a common purpose

294. **c.** nefarious means flagrantly wicked, or **evil**

295. **a.** to curry means to seek to gain favor, or to **flatter**

296. **b.** preternatural means exceeding what is natural, or **extraordinary**

297. **a.** pernicious means highly injurious or deadly, or **noxious**

298. **c.** a reprisal is an act of vengeance, or a **retaliation**

299. **c.** manifold means marked by variety, or **diverse**

300. **c.** factious means inclined to form factions; **seditious** means disposed to insurrection

Antonyms

Select the word that is most dissimilar in meaning to the word provided.

301. tragic
  a. boring
  b. mysterious
  c. comic
  d. incredulous

302. able
  a. willful
  b. inept
  c. careful
  d. feasible

303. tireless
  a. exhausted
  b. unfailing
  c. broke
  d. driving

304. wean
  a. flourish
  b. flush
  c. strengthen
  d. addict

305. haste
  a. delay
  b. frugal
  c. debauchery
  d. solemnity

306. malice
  a. goodwill
  b. bitterness
  c. coddle
  d. distress

307. permanent
　　a. loose
　　b. fierce
　　c. fleeting
　　d. unhappy

308. attain
　　a. crave
　　b. lose
　　c. harbor
　　d. credit

309. taint
　　a. cheer
　　b. worry
　　c. clear
　　d. purify

310. belittle
　　a. plain
　　b. detract
　　c. magnify
　　d. torment

311. tedious
　　a. unwavering
　　b. frightening
　　c. horrible
　　d. pleasurable

312. license
　　a. restriction
　　b. allow
　　c. join
　　d. gather

313. frivolous
　　a. pious
　　b. inexpensive
　　c. serious
　　d. contemptuous

314. plain
　　a. meadow
　　b. ugly
　　c. lovely
　　d. unadorned

315. denounce
　　a. covet
　　b. condemn
　　c. blame
　　d. deplore

316. contrary
　　a. urbane
　　b. agreeable
　　c. unpleasant
　　d. despicable

317. glower
　　a. prairie
　　b. smile
　　c. raise
　　d. throw

318. exacting
　　a. upright
　　b. lenient
　　c. sober
　　d. general

319. curtail
  a. remain
  b. detain
  c. placate
  d. prolong

320. eminent
  a. imminent
  b. obscure
  c. retire
  d. unsure

321. abdicate
  a. deny
  b. usurp
  c. blame
  d. renounce

322. indolent
  a. industrious
  b. complimentary
  c. native
  d. smooth

323. fortuitous
  a. undefended
  b. gratuitous
  c. deliberate
  d. impoverished

324. disparage
  a. hesitate
  b. settle
  c. trouble
  d. applaud

325. dubious
  a. reliable
  b. pleasing
  c. rhythmic
  d. careful

326. interdict
  a. continue
  b. abstain
  c. wallow
  d. sanction

327. mendacious
  a. bashful
  b. capacious
  c. veracious
  d. quiet

328. lassitude
  a. release
  b. demure
  c. fatigue
  d. vigor

329. verdant
  a. dishonest
  b. suspicious
  c. moldy
  d. arid

330. ductile
  a. unfeeling
  b. arrogant
  c. precious
  d. rigid

331. asperity
  a. moistness
  b. amenity
  c. sour
  d. generosity

332. epicurean
  a. ascetic
  b. slovenly
  c. imprecision
  d. providential

333. traduce
  a. deduce
  b. laud
  c. presuppose
  d. converge

334. bridle
  a. heckle
  b. dissuade
  c. vent
  d. persist

335. spare
  a. rotund
  b. pacify
  c. impolite
  d. impose

336. proclivity
  a. calm
  b. antipathy
  c. desire
  d. dearth

337. vituperation
  a. alacrity
  b. alertness
  c. reparation
  d. acclaim

338. gambol
  a. trudge
  b. hedge
  c. crone
  d. misplace

339. quixotic
  a. simple
  b. staid
  c. passe
  d. unpredictable

340. lachrymose
  a. quick
  b. loquacious
  c. blithe
  d. plentiful

Answers

301. **c.** tragic means regrettably serious or sorrowful; **comic** means humorous

302. **b.** able means having skill or ability; **inept** means lacking skill

303. **a.** tireless means filled with energy; **exhausted** means depleted of energy

304. **d.** to wean means to detach from a dependence; to **addict** means to make dependent

305. **a.** haste means hurry; **delay** means postponement or procrastination

306. **a.** malice means a desire to see another suffer; **goodwill** means desire to see another benefit

307. **c.** permanent means lasting; **fleeting** means passing quickly or temporary

308. **b.** to attain means to achieve or to gain, therefore to **lose** is the most dissimilar

309. **d.** to taint means to contaminate or corrupt; to **purify** means to make pure

310. **c.** to belittle means to make seem little or less; to **magnify** means to enlarge

311. **d.** tedious means boring; **pleasurable** means enjoyable or delightful

312. **a.** one meaning of a license is permission; **restriction** means limitation

313. **c.** frivolous means lacking seriousness, therefore **serious** is the most dissimilar

314. **c.** plain means lacking in beauty; **lovely** means beautiful

315. **a.** one meaning of to denounce is to speak out against; to **covet** means to wish for enviously

316. **b.** contrary means unwilling to accept control or advice; **agreeable** means ready or willing to agree

317. **b.** glower means a sullen brooding look, therefore **smile** is the most dissimilar

318. **b.** exacting means severe; **lenient** means indulgent

319. **d.** to curtail means to cut short; to **prolong** means to lengthen or extend

320. **b.** eminent means prominent, or famous; **obscure** means not prominent, or unknown

321. **b.** to abdicate means to renounce power or high office; to **usurp** means seize power or high office

322. **a.** indolent means lazy; **industrious** means hardworking

323. **c.** fortuitous means occurring by chance, or accidental; **deliberate** means resulting from careful consideration, or voluntary

324. **d.** to disparage means to speak slightingly about; to **applaud** means to express approval

325. **a.** dubious means questionable or unreliable, therefore **reliable** is the most dissimilar

326. **d.** to interdict means to forbid; to **sanction** means to approve

327. **c.** mendacious means dishonest; **veracious** means truthful or honest

328. **d.** lassitude means weariness; **vigor** means strength or force

329. **d.** one meaning of verdant is green, especially with plant life; **arid** means dry, or lacking enough rainfall for agriculture

330. **d.** one meaning of ductile is easily led or influenced; one meaning of **rigid** is inflexible, set in opinion

331. **b.** asperity means roughness of surface or manner; **amenity** means pleasantness or smoothness of manner

332. **a.** epicurean means having sensitive and self-indulgent taste especially in food and wine; **ascetic** means practicing self-denial and austerity

333. **b.** to traduce means to expose to shame or blame; to **laud** means to praise or extol

334. **c.** to bridle means to restrain or keep under control; to **vent** means to relieve by means of an outlet

335. **a.** one meaning of spare is lean; **rotund** means round or fleshy

336. **b.** proclivity means inclination or predisposition; **antipathy** means settled aversion or dislike

337. **d.** vituperation means bitter condemnation; **acclaim** means praise

338. **a.** to gambol means to skip about in play; to **trudge** means to march steadily and laboriously

339. **b.** quixotic means foolishly impractical and marked by extravagantly romantic ideals; **staid** means sedate and marked by prim self-restraint

340. **c.** lachrymose means given to weeping, or morose; **blithe** means of a happy or lighthearted character, or merry

10

Synonyms

Select the word that is closest in meaning to the word provided.

341. glare is most similar to
   a. scowl
   b. hide
   c. display
   d. summon

342. erratic is most similar to
   a. enticing
   b. frequent
   c. difficult
   d. irregular

343. civil is most similar to
   a. unkind
   b. trite
   c. public
   d. questionable

344. peer is most similar to
   a. apple
   b. connote
   c. fellow
   d. recluse

345. fiasco is most similar to
   a. festival
   b. disaster
   c. happenstance
   d. ceremony

346. chasm is most similar to
   a. gorge
   b. charm
   c. bridle
   d. criticize

347. expertise is most similar to
  a. activity
  b. courage
  c. mastery
  d. effort

348. outlandish is most similar to
  a. distant
  b. absurd
  c. pastoral
  d. belligerent

349. pine is most similar to
  a. clean
  b. hate
  c. resolve
  d. crave

350. exploit is most similar to
  a. answer
  b. feat
  c. accident
  d. persuade

351. culmination is most similar to
  a. realization
  b. disaster
  c. serendipity
  d. persuasion

352. feign is most similar to
  a. jab
  b. swoon
  c. pretend
  d. dread

353. auspicious is most similar to
  a. deceitful
  b. foreboding
  c. favorable
  d. dangerous

354. gambit is most similar to
  a. frolic
  b. ploy
  c. testimony
  d. sentence

355. voracious is most similar to
  a. ravenous
  b. violent
  c. voluble
  d. rambunctious

356. facile is most similar to
  a. ability
  b. section
  c. vindictive
  d. glib

357. eschew is most similar to
  a. revert
  b. accompany
  c. admire
  d. abstain

358. abscond is most similar to
  a. rob
  b. obscure
  c. flee
  d. absolve

359. knack is most similar to
    a. bruise
    b. ability
    c. keepsake
    d. scoundrel

360. apropos is most similar to
    a. opportune
    b. unexpected
    c. misspoken
    d. idea

361. veritable is most similar to
    a. deep
    b. authentic
    c. ancient
    d. irascible

362. unmitigated is most similar to
    a. audacious
    b. unpersuasive
    c. utter
    d. dense

363. epitome is most similar to
    a. volume
    b. essence
    c. summit
    d. deliverance

364. edict is most similar to
    a. decree
    b. vacate
    c. correction
    d. destiny

365. extol is most similar to
    a. praise
    b. tax
    c. burden
    d. berate

366. abeyant is most similar to
    a. false
    b. disgusting
    c. pending
    d. novice

367. knell is most similar to
    a. copse
    b. hill
    c. toll
    d. rattle

368. soporific is most similar to
    a. juvenile
    b. drunken
    c. delightful
    d. hypnotic

369. iterate is most similar to
    a. unsettled
    b. repeat
    c. impoverish
    d. announce

370. bulwark is most similar to
    a. conundrum
    b. festival
    c. rampart
    d. confuse

371. pedantic is most similar to
   a. pedestrian
   b. arduous
   c. fickle
   d. consequential

372. bumptious is most similar to
   a. backward
   b. arrogant
   c. clumsy
   d. rugged

373. expiation is most similar to
   a. breathing
   b. immigration
   c. divergence
   d. atonement

374. flagitious is most similar to
   a. deliberate
   b. fatiguing
   c. villainous
   d. habitual

375. inveigle is most similar to
   a. cajole
   b. complexity
   c. hoodwink
   d. distress

Answers

341. **a.** to glare means to stare angrily; to **scowl** means to have an angry expression

342. **d.** erratic means lacking regularity, or **irregular**

343. **c.** one meaning of civil is involving the general **public**

344. **c.** a peer is a person belonging to the same group; a **fellow** is an equal in rank, or a member of the same group

345. **b.** a fiasco is a complete failure, or a **disaster**

346. **a.** a chasm is a deep split in the earth, or a **gorge**

347. **c.** expertise and **mastery** both mean special skills or knowledge

348. **b.** outlandish means extremely out of the ordinary; **absurd** means ridiculously unreasonable

349. **d.** to pine means to long for, or to **crave**

350. **b.** an exploit is a notable or heroic act; a **feat** is a courageous deed

351. **a.** culmination means the act of reaching the highest point, or decisive action; **realization** means the act of bringing into concrete existence

352. **c.** to feign means to assert as if true, or to **pretend**

353. **c.** auspicious means marked by **favorable** signs

354. **b.** one meaning of gambit is a calculated move; a **ploy** is a tactic

355. **a.** voracious and **ravenous** mean having a huge appetite

356. **d.** facile means easily achieved and often lacking sincerity; **glib** means marked by ease and lacking depth and substance

357. **d.** to eschew means to avoid habitually, or to **abstain**

358. **c.** to abscond means to depart secretly; to **flee** means to run away

359. **b.** a knack is a special **ability**

360. **a.** apropos means being both relevant and appropriate; **opportune** means occurring at an appropriate time

361. **b.** veritable means not false or imagined, or **authentic**

362. **c.** unmitigated means offering little chance of change or relief, or absolute; **utter** means total or absolute

363. **b.** an epitome is a typical or ideal example; **essence** is the real or very basic nature of something

364. **a.** an edict is an official proclamation; a **decree** is an order with the force of the law

365. **a.** to extol means to **praise** highly

366. **c.** abeyant means in a period of temporary inactivity, or **pending**

367. **c.** to knell means to sound in an ominous manner; to **toll** means to sound in long measured strokes; both words are used to describe the ringing of bells

368. **d.** soporific means causing sleep; **hypnotic** means tending to produce sleep

369. **b.** to iterate means to say or do again, or to **repeat**

370. **c.** a bulwark is a solid wall-like structure raised for defense, or a **rampart**

371. **a.** pedantic means ostentatiously or narrowly learned, or unimaginative; one meaning of **pedestrian** is commonplace or unimaginative

372. **b.** bumptious means noisily self-assertive; **arrogant** means disposed to exaggerate one's own worth

373. **d.** expiation means the act of making atonement; **atonement** means reparation for an offense or injury

374. **c.** flagitious means marked by outrageous crime or vice; **villainous** means having the characteristics of a deliberate criminal or scoundrel

375. **a.** to inveigle means to win over with flattery; to **cajole** means to persuade with flattery

11

Antonyms

Select the word that is most dissimilar in meaning to the word provided.

376. prudent is most dissimilar to
- **a.** simple
- **b.** rapid
- **c.** foolish
- **d.** verbose

377. forced is most dissimilar to
- **a.** quick
- **b.** solid
- **c.** trusting
- **d.** natural

378. acquaint is most dissimilar to
- **a.** alienate
- **b.** luxurious
- **c.** bleach
- **d.** stall

379. expansive is most dissimilar to
- **a.** generous
- **b.** honest
- **c.** narrow
- **d.** troublesome

380. benign is most dissimilar to
- **a.** malignant
- **b.** converse
- **c.** cautious
- **d.** malicious

381. foster is most dissimilar to
- **a.** discourage
- **b.** believe
- **c.** heal
- **d.** brag

382. ample is most dissimilar to
  a. complete
  b. insufficient
  c. quiet
  d. supple

383. deviant is most dissimilar to
  a. winding
  b. careful
  c. normal
  d. sad

384. abolish is most dissimilar to
  a. vote
  b. punish
  c. avoid
  d. establish

385. forsake is most dissimilar to
  a. craft
  b. embrace
  c. shun
  d. infer

386. tractable is most dissimilar to
  a. invisible
  b. stubborn
  c. unadvisable
  d. special

387. dexterous is most dissimilar to
  a. clumsy
  b. saline
  c. cunning
  d. precious

388. aerate is most dissimilar to
  a. argue
  b. placate
  c. suffocate
  d. destroy

389. venerable is most dissimilar to
  a. impervious
  b. constant
  c. sophomoric
  d. infirm

390. rancor is most dissimilar to
  a. ritual
  b. argument
  c. collect
  d. accord

391. daunt is most dissimilar to
  a. calm
  b. believe
  c. inspirit
  d. dispel

392. paucity is most dissimilar to
  a. excess
  b. certainty
  c. timidity
  d. beauty

393. heedless is most dissimilar to
  a. heartless
  b. attentive
  c. speedy
  d. unaware

394. abound is most dissimilar to
a. rest
b. discourage
c. bless
d. dwindle

395. confederate is most
dissimilar to
a. enemy
b. confuse
c. wander
d. cluster

396. resplendent is most
dissimilar to
a. illuminated
b. disarming
c. dowdy
d. delightful

397. onerous is most dissimilar to
a. permissive
b. easy
c. unforgiving
d. public

398. sagacity is most dissimilar to
a. incredulity
b. belligerence
c. stupidity
d. tolerance

399. dilettante is most dissimilar to
a. puritan
b. professional
c. aesthete
d. conniver

400. unalloyed is most
dissimilar to
a. dismayed
b. impure
c. circumspect
d. disastrous

401. banner is most dissimilar to
a. forgettable
b. casual
c. unrestrained
d. unwitting

402. discalced is most dissimilar to
a. calculated
b. measured
c. inclined
d. shod

403. scurrilous is most
dissimilar to
a. honest
b. decent
c. peaceful
d. satisfactory

404. pulchritudinous is most
dissimilar to
a. pacifist
b. rare
c. smooth
d. unsightly

405. dyspeptic is most dissimilar to
a. trusting
b. functional
c. euphoric
d. talented

406. reliction is most dissimilar to
    a. dedication
    b. demolition
    c. flood
    d. problem

407. villenage is most dissimilar to
    a. nobility
    b. lineage
    c. directness
    d. dullness

408. craven is most dissimilar to
    a. stalwart
    b. release
    c. distinguished
    d. comfortable

409. prolix is most dissimilar to
    a. brief
    b. exquisite
    c. reasonable
    d. distinct

410. lambent is most dissimilar to
    a. praise
    b. present
    c. dull
    d. rough

Answers

376. **c.** prudent means marked by wisdom or good judgment; **foolish** means marked by a lack of good sense or prudence

377. **d.** forced means produced with effort; **natural** means uncultivated or spontaneous

378. **a.** to acquaint means to get to know or to become friendly; to **alienate** means to cause unfriendliness or hostility

379. **c.** expansive means sizeable or extensive; **narrow** means restricted

380. **d.** one meaning of benign is of a gentle disposition; **malicious** means marked by mischievous impulse

381. **a.** to foster means to encourage; to **discourage** means to deprive of courage or confidence

382. **b.** ample means more than adequate in size, scope, or capacity, or sufficient, therefore, **insufficient** is the most dissimilar

383. **c.** deviant means departing from the established norm, or abnormal, therefore **normal** is the most dissimilar

384. **d.** to abolish means to do away with entirely; to **establish** means to bring into existence

385. **b.** to forsake means to renounce; one meaning of to **embrace** is to welcome or include

386. **b.** tractable means easily handled or managed; **stubborn** means difficult to handle or manage

387. **a.** dexterous means skillful with the hands; **clumsy** means lacking dexterity, nimbleness, or grace

388. **c.** to aerate means to supply with oxygen; to **suffocate** means to deprive of oxygen

389. **c.** venerable means impressive by reason of age; **sophomoric** means poorly informed and immature

390. **d.** rancor means bitter ill-will; one meaning of **accord** is balanced interrelationship, or harmony

391. **c.** to daunt means to lessen the courage of; to **inspirit** means to give vigor or courage

392. **a.** paucity means smallness of number; **excess** means ample quantity

393. **b.** heedless means inconsiderate or thoughtless; **attentive** means heedful or mindful of the comfort of others

394. **d.** to abound means to be present in great numbers; to **dwindle** means to become steadily less

395. **a.** a confederate is an ally or accomplice; an **enemy** is an opponent

396. **c.** resplendent means characterized by glowing splendor; **dowdy** means not neat or attractive in appearance, or shabby

397. **b.** onerous means burdensome or troublesome, therefore **easy** is the most dissimilar

398. **c.** sagacity means wisdom; **stupidity** means a lack of wisdom

399. **b.** a dilettante is a person having a superficial interest in an art or branch or knowledge; a **professional** is a person who engages in a pursuit as a profession

400. **b.** unalloyed means pure, therefore **impure** is the most dissimilar

401. **a.** banner means distinguished from all others in excellence, or unforgettable, therefore **forgettable** is the most dissimilar

402. **d.** discalced means barefoot; **shod** means wearing shoes

403. **b.** scurrilous means given to using foul language, or crass; **decent** means conforming to standards of propriety

404. **d.** pulchritudinous means marked by physical beauty; **unsightly** means not pleasing to the sight, or ugly

405. **c.** dyspeptic means showing a sour disposition; **euphoric** means marked by feeling or well-being

406. **c.** reliction means the gradual recession of water leaving the land dry; **flood** means the rising and overflow of a body of water onto dry land

407. **a.** villenage means the peasant or commoner class; **nobility** means the noble class, or gentry

408. **a.** craven means cowardly; **stalwart** means marked by outstanding strength or vigor

409. **a.** prolix means unduly prolonged, therefore **brief** is the most dissimilar

410. **c.** lambent means softly bright or radiant; **dull** means lacking in brightness or shine

12

Synonyms

Select the word that is most similar in meaning to the word provided.

411. heed
  a. trek
  b. consider
  c. consolidate
  d. bound

412. edge
  a. diffuse
  b. point
  c. force
  d. dissuade

413. elevate
  a. lessen
  b. mention
  c. affix
  d. hoist

414. appoint
  a. score
  b. discuss
  c. nominate
  d. ensure

415. hoard
  a. stockpile
  b. burrow
  c. mine
  d. dessert

416. homogeneous
  a. alike
  b. strange
  c. polite
  d. alkaline

417. hub
   a. counsel
   b. elder
   c. center
   d. extension

418. tame
   a. lost
   b. evasive
   c. pushy
   d. submissive

419. irk
   a. shrug
   b. irritate
   c. devour
   d. avoid

420. loom
   a. disappear
   b. cut
   c. surface
   d. teach

421. fitful
   a. erratic
   b. angry
   c. tired
   d. pronounced

422. gaudy
   a. massive
   b. mindful
   c. tasteful
   d. flashy

423. flaunt
   a. conceal
   b. parade
   c. trust
   d. fray

424. flex
   a. bend
   b. binge
   c. rid
   d. consume

425. tantalize
   a. pronounce
   b. reign
   c. equal
   d. flirt

426. dastardly
   a. devastating
   b. cowardly
   c. clever
   d. munificent

427. aficionado
   a. novice
   b. trickster
   c. devotee
   d. agent

428. contiguous
   a. catching
   b. divided
   c. adjoining
   d. circumstantial

429. swindler
 a. charlatan
 b. expert
 c. divinity
 d. debonair

430. rogue
 a. knave
 b. wander
 c. buffoon
 d. color

431. apologist
 a. liar
 b. defender
 c. failure
 d. admirer

432. proxy
 a. spasm
 b. closeness
 c. delegate
 d. court

433. buffet
 a. protect
 b. barricade
 c. armoire
 d. strike

434. travesty
 a. confusion
 b. mockery
 c. disaster
 d. speculation

435. bristle
 a. aloof
 b. seethe
 c. wave
 d. doubt

436. admonish
 a. laud
 b. decorate
 c. caution
 d. admire

437. wheedle
 a. retreat
 b. deceive
 c. plead
 d. question

438. aplomb
 a. mine
 b. clumsiness
 c. complication
 d. poise

439. aver
 a. dissipate
 b. create
 c. hate
 d. state

440. mien
 a. carriage
 b. average
 c. vicious
 d. disguise

441. paroxysm
  a. conundrum
  b. fit
  c. contraction
  d. spite

442. aegis
  a. superstition
  b. reference
  c. sponsorship
  d. archive

443. sepulture
  a. burial
  b. parasite
  c. verse
  d. sermon

444. harridan
  a. governor
  b. vessel
  c. witch
  d. lawyer

445. apothegm
  a. medicine
  b. adage
  c. speculation
  d. resistance

446. grandiloquence
  a. respect
  b. bluster
  c. denial
  d. solemnity

447. fulmination
  a. explosion
  b. recession
  c. achievement
  d. blessing

448. pococurante
  a. native
  b. hot
  c. blasé
  d. hidden

449. escarpment
  a. warning
  b. cliff
  c. campsite
  d. tomb

450. plutocrat
  a. banker
  b. priest
  c. judge
  d. astronomer

Answers

411. **b.** to heed means to pay attention to, or to **consider**

412. **a.** to edge means to **force** or move gradually (as in to edge off the road)

413. **d.** to elevate means to lift up, or raise; to **hoist** means to raise into position

414. **c.** to appoint means to name officially, often to a position; to **nominate** means to appoint or propose for office

415. **a.** to hoard means to gather a hidden supply; to **stockpile** means accumulate a reserve of something

416. **a.** homogeneous means descended from the same ancestral type, or **alike**

417. **c.** a hub is a **center** of activity

418. **d.** tame means deficient in spirit or courage, or **submissive**

419. **b.** to irk means to annoy or **irritate**

420. **c.** to loom means to come into sight in enlarged or distorted form; to **surface** means to come to the surface or into view

421. **a.** fitful means having intermittent or irregular character; **erratic** means lacking regularity

422. **d.** gaudy means ostentatiously or tastelessly ornamented; **flashy** means ostentatious or showy

423. **b.** to flaunt means to display ostentatiously or impudently; to **parade** means to exhibit ostentatiously

424. **a.** to flex means to **bend**

425. **d.** to tantalize means to tease by presenting something desirable; to **flirt** means to behave amorously without serious intent

426. **b.** dastardly means despicably mean or **cowardly**

427. **c.** an aficionado is a fan, or a **devotee**

428. **c.** contiguous means touching along a boundary or point; **adjoining** means joining at a point or line

429. **a.** a swindler is a person who takes money or property through fraud or deceit; a **charlatan** is a person who pretends to have knowledge or ability, or a fraud

430. **a.** a rogue is a dishonest person; a **knave** is a tricky deceitful person

431. **b.** an apologist is a person who writes or speaks in defense of a cause, or a **defender**

432. **c.** a proxy is a person who has the power to act for another, or a **delegate**

433. **d.** to buffet means to **strike** repeatedly

434. **b.** a travesty is a distorted or grossly inferior imitation; a **mockery** is an insincere or contemptible imitation

435. **b.** to bristle is to take on an aggressive or angry appearance; to **seethe** means to experience violent internal agitation

436. **c.** to admonish means to express warning in a gentle manner, or to **caution**

437. **c.** to wheedle means to influence using soft words or flattery; to **plead** means to entreat or appeal earnestly

438. **d.** aplomb means complete composure or self-assurance, or **poise**

439. **d.** to aver means to declare positively, or to **state**

440. **a.** mien means appearance or demeanor; **carriage** means manner of holding one's body, or posture

441. **b.** a paroxysm is an attack or convulsion, or a **fit**

442. **c.** aegis means protection, or **sponsorship**

443. **a.** sepulture means **burial**

444. **c.** a harridan is a shrew, or a **witch**

445. **b.** an apothegm is a short, pithy saying; an **adage** is a saying that embodies a common observation

446. **b.** grandiloquence means lofty or pompous eloquence; one meaning of **bluster** is loudly boastful speech

447. **a.** a fulmination is a sudden or loud noise, or an **explosion**

448. **c.** pococurante means indifferent or nonchalant; **blasé** means apathetic to pleasure

449. **b.** an escarpment is a long **cliff** or a steep slope

450. **a.** a plutocrat is one who rules by virtue of wealth; a **banker** is one who engages in the business of finance

13

Antonyms

Select the word that is most dissimilar in meaning to the word provided.

451. subsequent
  a. aloof
  b. previous
  c. following
  d. dismissive

452. abrupt
  a. continue
  b. laudable
  c. anticipated
  d. careless

453. conserve
  a. waste
  b. silence
  c. liberal
  d. complicate

454. waive
  a. retain
  b. snub
  c. imprison
  d. display

455. erode
  a. compost
  b. clarify
  c. ignore
  d. restore

456. recall
  a. rebate
  b. demonstrate
  c. forget
  d. despise

457. dormant
   a. clever
   b. active
   c. dreamy
   d. invisible

458. procrastinate
   a. lengthen
   b. soothe
   c. hurry
   d. demolish

459. docile
   a. intelligent
   b. unruly
   c. unreachable
   d. pale

460. impromptu
   a. rehearsed
   b. bizarre
   c. foolish
   d. disarming

461. denigrate
   a. blame
   b. hide
   c. query
   d. uphold

462. bent
   a. curved
   b. disinclination
   c. careful
   d. lustrous

463. solvent
   a. soggy
   b. confusing
   c. broke
   d. critical

464. disconsolate
   a. joyful
   b. inhospitable
   c. anguished
   d. rude

465. brusque
   a. cold
   b. opulent
   c. gracious
   d. suspect

466. callow
   a. kind
   b. urbane
   c. sensitive
   d. gentle

467. countenance
   a. force
   b. genuine
   c. deny
   d. verify

468. cachet
   a. release
   b. explanation
   c. thinness
   d. ignominy

469. evince
   a. convince
   b. hallow
   c. hide
   d. interpret

470. vainglorious
   a. horrible
   b. fierce
   c. greedy
   d. modest

471. iniquitous
   a. virtuous
   b. complacent
   c. equal
   d. virulent

472. obstreperous
   a. short
   b. tame
   c. strict
   d. distant

473. ebullient
   a. aggressive
   b. acrid
   c. unjust
   d. glum

474. halcyon
   a. obtrusive
   b. advanced
   c. tempestuous
   d. unscientific

475. imprimatur
   a. servant
   b. teacher
   c. disapproval
   d. rustic

476. odium
   a. fragrance
   b. ease
   c. admiration
   d. trust

477. mephitic
   a. honest
   b. healthy
   c. simple
   d. rural

478. platitudinous
   a. hilly
   b. exhilarating
   c. confounded
   d. advantageous

479. facultative
   a. compulsory
   b. insipid
   c. pending
   d. decisive

480. persiflage
   a. coddle
   b. admiration
   c. silence
   d. clarity

Answers

451. **b.** subsequent means following in time or order; **previous** means going before in time or order

452. **c.** abrupt means occurring without warning, or sudden; **anticipated** means expected

453. **a.** to conserve means to keep safe or preserve, which is the opposite of to **waste**

454. **a.** to waive means to give up voluntarily; to **retain** means to keep

455. **d.** to erode means to wear away; to **restore** means to bring back to an original state

456. **c.** to recall means to remember, which is the opposite of to **forget**

457. **b.** dormant means temporarily inactive, which is the opposite of **active**

458. **c.** to procrastinate means to delay or put off, which is the opposite of to **hurry**

459. **b.** docile means easily taught; **unruly** means not easily managed or disciplined

460. **a.** impromptu means unplanned or unrehearsed; **rehearsed** means trained or practiced

461. **d.** to denigrate means to deny the importance of something, or to belittle; to **uphold** means to support or to elevate

462. **b.** a bent is a strong inclination or capacity; a **disinclination** is a slight aversion

463. **c.** one meaning of solvent is able to pay all debts; **broke** means penniless

464. **a.** disconsolate means cheerless or dejected, which is the opposite of **joyful**

465. **c.** brusque means blunt in manner or speech to the point of being ungracious; **gracious** means marked by charm and good taste

466. **b.** callow means unsophisticated; **urbane** means sophisticated

467. **c.** to countenance means to extend approval or sanction; to **deny** means to refuse to grant

468. **d.** cachet means prestige; **ignominy** means disgrace

469. **c.** to evince means to display clearly or reveal, which is the opposite of to **hide**

470. **d.** vainglorious means boastful, which is the opposite of **modest**

471. **a.** iniquitous means wicked; **virtuous** means morally excellent

472. **b.** obstreperous means stubbornly resistant to control or unruly; **tame** means docile or submissive

473. **d.** ebullient means lively or enthusiastic; **glum** means dreary or gloomy

474. **c.** halcyon means calm or peaceful; **tempestuous** means turbulent or stormy

475. **c.** imprimatur means sanction or approval, therefore **disapproval** is the most dissimilar

476. **c.** odium means hatred and condemnation; **admiration** means a feeling of delighted approval

477. **b.** mephitic means relating to a foul, noxious exhalation from the earth; a mephitic environment would be unhealthy, so **healthy** is its opposite

478. **b.** platitudinous means full of or characterized by banal, trite remarks; **exhilarating** means refreshing or exciting

479. **a.** facultative means optional; **compulsory** means mandatory, or not optional

480. **c.** persiflage means frivolous talk, therefore **silence** is the most dissimilar

14

Synonyms and Antonyms

Read each question carefully and select the word that is the most similar or most dissimilar in meaning to the word provided.

481. beckon is most similar to
  a. light
  b. beg
  c. motion
  d. hear

482. earnest is most dissimilar to
  a. cheap
  b. frivolous
  c. release
  d. civilized

483. execute is most similar to
  a. perform
  b. decide
  c. wonder
  d. dismiss

484. idiom is most similar to
  a. stupidity
  b. recipe
  c. fastener
  d. expression

485. accelerate is most dissimilar to
  a. delay
  b. risk
  c. monitor
  d. deny

486. engross is most similar to
  a. fatten
  b. absorb
  c. disgust
  d. destroy

487. impervious is most dissimilar to
a. kind
b. disastrous
c. prone
d. perfect

488. brood is most similar to
a. wander
b. direction
c. progeny
d. tribe

489. balk is most similar to
a. crow
b. fight
c. distress
d. hamper

490. conversant is most dissimilar to
a. inexperienced
b. unprepared
c. shy
d. unpretentious

491. staunch is most similar to
a. faithful
b. strict
c. biased
d. political

492. unctuous is most dissimilar to
a. pliant
b. cruel
c. sincere
d. rubbery

493. hubris is most similar to
a. earth
b. pride
c. humility
d. sorrow

494. bemuse is most dissimilar to
a. depress
b. inspire
c. clarify
d. desire

495. contrite is most similar to
a. brief
b. malicious
c. banal
d. rueful

496. beset is most similar to
a. hector
b. decorate
c. establish
d. suspect

497. penurious is most dissimilar to
a. generous
b. lenient
c. injurious
d. relaxed

498. perfidy is most similar to
a. incompleteness
b. ideal
c. betrayal
d. braggart

499. ascription is most similar to
    a. account
    b. attribution
    c. cure
    d. description

500. fustigate is most dissimilar to
    a. inveigle
    b. investigate
    c. explain
    d. praise

501. bagatelle is most similar to
    a. paste
    b. bread
    c. bauble
    d. pirouette

Answers

481. **c.** to beckon means to signal or summon with a wave or a nod; to **motion** means to gesture

482. **b.** earnest means grave or serious; **frivolous** means lacking in seriousness

483. **a.** one meaning of to execute is to carry out fully; one meaning of to **perform** is to carry out

484. **d.** an idiom is an **expression** that is unique either grammatically or in meaning

485. **a.** to accelerate means to cause to move faster; to **delay** means to move or act slowly

486. **b.** to engross means to occupy completely; one meaning of to **absorb** is to engage or engross wholly

487. **c.** impervious means to be incapable of being affected or disturbed; **prone** means having a tendency or inclination, or being likely

488. **c.** a brood is the young of an animal or a family of young; **progeny** is the offspring of animals or plants

489. **d.** one meaning of to balk is to check or to stop; to **hamper** means to impede or restrain

490. **a.** conversant means having knowledge or experience with, therefore **inexperienced** is the most dissimilar

491. **a.** staunch means steadfast in loyalty or principle, or **faithful**

492. **c.** unctuous means marked by a smug or false earnestness, or insincere, therefore **sincere** is the most dissimilar

493. **b.** hubris means exaggerated **pride** or self-confidence

494. **c.** to bemuse means to make confused, or to bewilder; to **clarify** means to make free from confusion

495. **d.** contrite means penitent for sin or failing; **rueful** means regretful

496. **a.** to beset means to trouble or harass; to **hector** means to intimidate or harass

497. **a.** penurious means given to extreme stinginess or frugality, which is the opposite of **generous**

498. **c.** perfidy means an act of disloyalty, or **betrayal**

499. **b.** ascription means the act of referring to a supposed cause, source, or author; **attribution** means the act of explaining by indicating a cause, or the act of ascribing a work to a particular author or artist

500. **d.** to fustigate means to criticize severely, which is the opposite of to **praise**

501. **c.** a bagatelle is a trifle (something of little value or importance); a **bauble** is a trinket or a trifle

SKILL BUILDER IN FOCUS

ISBN: 1-57685-422-1
128 pages
7 x 10
AUGUST 2002

501 Word Analogy Questions

Master this logic and reasoning skill and score higher!

Achieve maximum results with proven practice

Build test-taking confidence—fast

Great for the SAT, GRE, GMAT—and other standardized tests

**Pinpoint exact word definitions and
become aware of secondary word meanings**

**Deduce the correct relationship between words and draw
logical conclusions about possible answer choices**

**Learn to identify types of analogies—cause/effect, part/whole,
type/category, synonym, antonym, word knowledge,
and more—to avoid careless mistakes**

**Assess your true ability to apply logic and reasoning skills to
word knowledge and put yourself on the path to improvement**

Focus *FAST* on Word Analogies

SKILL BUILDER IN FOCUS

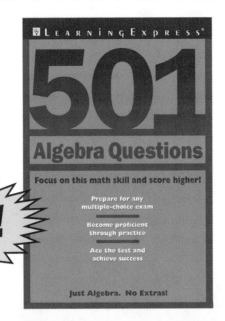

ISBN: 1-57685-424-8
288 pages
7 x 10
AUGUST 2002

501 Algebra Questions

Master this math skill and score higher!

Achieve maximum results with proven practice

Build test-taking confidence—fast

**Great practice for the SAT, GRE, GMAT—
and other standardized tests**

Learn math concepts and properties

Work with algebraic expressions and integers

**Multiply and factor polynomials, use quadratic
formulas, and avoid careless mistakes**

**Assess your true algebra competency level
and put yourself on the path to improvement**

Focus *FAST* on Algebra

SKILL BUILDER IN FOCUS

ISBN: 1-57685-425-6
288 pages
7 x 10
AUGUST 2002

501 Geometry Questions

Master this math skill and score higher!

Achieve maximum results with proven practice

Build test-taking confidence—fast

**Great for the SAT, GRE, GMAT—
and other standardized tests**

**Learn math concepts and properties,
including trigonometry basics**

**Work with angles and lines, identify shapes,
determine ratios, proportion, perimeter,
and surface measures**

**Assess your true geometry competency level
and put yourself on the path to improvement**

Focus *FAST* on Geometry

SKILL BUILDER IN FOCUS
coming in Winter 2003

501 Quantitative Comparison Questions
ISBN: 1-57685-434-5 ▪ 224 pages ▪ 7 x 10 ▪ January

501 Writing Prompts
ISBN: 1-57685-438-8 ▪ 128 pages ▪ 7 x 10 ▪ February

501 Math Word Problems
ISBN: 1-57685-439-6 ▪ 224 pages ▪ 7 x 10 ▪ March

Master these skills and score higher!

Achieve maximum results with proven practice

Build test-taking confidence—fast

**Great for the SAT, GRE, GMAT—
and other standardized tests**

Focus *FAST* on the Skills You Need to Pass the Test